扫描文章前的二维码
收听该故事的英文音频

"伟人的少年故事"丛书

天地的秘密

—— 观察星星和石头的科学家 ——

(斯里兰卡)努雷·维塔奇(Nury Vittachi) 著
斯泰帕·张(Step Cheung) 图
朱之翀 译 张群 审校

上海科技教育出版社

图书在版编目(CIP)数据

天地的秘密:观察星星和石头的科学家/(斯里)努雷·维塔奇(Nury Vittachi)著;朱之翀译.—上海:上海科技教育出版社,2018.8

("伟人的少年故事"丛书)

书名原文:Secrets in the Rocks

ISBN 978-7-5428-6707-0

I.①天… II.①努… ②朱… III.①科学家—生平事迹—世界—青少年读物 IV.①K816.1—49

中国版本图书馆CIP数据核字(2018)第069133号

Contents

Mary Anning The Girl Who Found a Flying Dragon   3

Georges Cuvier The Boy Who Went Searching for Giants   11

Mary Morland Love, Rocks and the First Dinosaur   19

Louis Agassiz The Bug Boy Solves a Huge Mystery   27

Inge Lehmann The Woman Who Saw Deep into the Earth   35

Jeremiah Horrocks The Boy Who Decoded the Dance of the Stars   43

Zhang Heng The Poet-Scientist Who Detected an Earthquake   51

Vesto Slipher The Farm Boy Who Saw the Galaxies Flying Away   58

Annie Jump Cannon The Girl Who Named the Stars in the Sky   67

Michio Kaku The Boy Who Understood Einstein   73

目录

玛丽·安宁　发现飞龙的女孩　3

乔治·居维叶　寻找巨人的男孩　11

玛丽·莫兰　爱、岩石和第一只恐龙　19

路易斯·阿加西　揭开巨大谜团的昆虫男孩　27

英奇·莱曼　了解地球深处的女子　35

杰里迈亚·霍罗克斯　破译星星舞蹈的男孩　43

张衡　感测地震的诗人兼科学家　51

维斯托·斯里弗　看到星系飞移的农场男孩　58

安妮·强普·坎农　为星星命名的女孩　67

加来道雄　理解爱因斯坦的男孩　73

THE GIRL WHO FOUND A FLYING DRAGON

玛丽·安宁
发现飞龙的女孩

LITTLE MARY SEEMED TO BE **destined**① for nothing but an early death.

She was born in a very poor family in the UK a little over 200 years ago. They had very little to eat and the only home they could afford was on the edge of the sea, near a dangerous cliff. No one else wanted to live there.

One by one, all her **siblings**② had died except her brother Joseph. Her father, Richard Anning, a carpenter, was sick and dying, too.

The home of the Anning family was not just damp, but sometimes flooded so badly that they needed to climb out of an upstairs window to avoid **drowning**③.

So Mary would leave her home and **explore**④ the **cliffs**⑤, which contained some beautiful patterned rocks — although the cliff walls were very **crumbly**⑥, and there were sometimes **landslides**⑦ which killed visitors.

Her chances of survival were very low.

Then her father finally died and the last three members of the family realized that they did not have enough money to survive.

年幼的玛丽似乎命中注定将红颜薄命。

200多年前，玛丽出生于英国一个极其贫困的家庭。他们经常吃了上顿没下顿，唯一住得起的房子位于海边一处险象环生的悬崖上，其他人都不愿意住在那里。

她的兄弟姐妹一个个相继夭折，只剩下她和哥哥约瑟夫。她的父亲理查德·安宁（Richard Anning）是一位木匠，也患上了重病，奄奄一息。

安宁一家的房子很潮湿，不仅如此，有时还会被海水淹没。这时候他们不得不从开在高处的窗户爬出，以免淹死。

每逢这时，玛丽会离开家，去探索悬崖上的奥秘——那里有许多刻有美丽图案的石头。崖壁很容易被踩碎，而且时常会发生山崩，导致游客遇难。

可以说，玛丽活下来的可能性很低。

她的父亲最后还是去世了，家中仅剩下三个人了。他们还意识到，手上的钱已无法维持日后的生活。

---

① **destine**［'destɪn］*vt.* 注定、命定、预定［destined, destined, destining］
② **sibling**［'sɪblɪŋ］*n.* 兄弟姐妹
③ **drown**［draʊn］*vt.* 淹没、把……淹死；*vi.* 淹死、溺死
④ **explore**［ɪk'splɔː; ek-］*vt.* 探索、探测、探险；*vi.* 探索、探测、探险
　［explored, explored, exploring］
⑤ **cliff**［klɪf］*n.* 悬崖、绝壁
⑥ **crumbly**［'krʌmblɪ］*adj.* 脆的、易碎的［crumblier, crumbliest］
⑦ **landslide**［'læn(d)slaɪd］*n.* 山崩，大胜利；*vi.* 发生山崩，以压倒优势获胜

The local church gave Mary and her mother and brother cash to buy food, and taught the children how to read and write. This bought them some time and gave them hope. But it turned out that the lethal seaside cliff where they lived would save their lives!

The strange, patterned rocks turned out to be **fossils**①: remains of prehistoric animals or plants, preserved in rock. Mary and her mother and brother searched for fossils and made a little money selling them to collectors and museums. In those days, the world's top science **community**② was a group of men in the UK, mostly churchmen. They arranged for her fossils to be **displayed**③ and raised money for the poor family.

They were wise to put their trust in the Annings. One day Mary found some big fossils of animals that few people had ever seen before.

One of them was put into a museum under the name "Flying Dragon". It was an ancient dinosaur with huge, bat-like wings. (Today we call these **creatures**④ **pterosaurs**⑤: dinosaur-era creatures which could fly like birds.)

Mary and her best friend, a little dog called Tray, also found the first **ichthyosaur**⑥: a creature which is shaped like a dolphin but is an ancient swimming reptile with sharp teeth.

当地的教堂为玛丽、她的母亲和哥哥提供资助,为他们购买食物,还教她和哥哥读书识字。这为他们争取了一些时间,也给他们带来了希望。不过他们后来发现,最终拯救了他们的,却是他们居住处的悬崖峭壁。

那种有着奇怪花纹的石头被证实是化石!这些石头内部保存着史前动植物的残骸。玛丽、玛丽母亲和哥哥三人到处寻找这种化石,并将它们卖给私人收藏家和博物馆,通过这种方式赚了些钱。当时世界上最顶尖的科学家协会都在英国,而其中大多数成员都是教徒。他们将玛丽一家发现的化石进行展示,并以此为贫困家庭筹集善款。

科学家们对安宁一家很信任,而此举最终也被证明是明智的。有一天,玛丽发现了一些以前几乎从来没人见过的大型动物化石。

其中一块化石被一家博物馆收藏了,并将其命名为"飞龙"。这是一种古代的恐龙,长着巨大的蝙蝠似的翅膀。(如今我们把这种生物叫作"翼龙",这是一种生活在恐龙时代、可以像鸟儿一样飞行的生物。)

除此之外,玛丽还和她最好的伙伴——一只名叫"托盘"的小狗,发现了第一个鱼龙化石。鱼龙是古代的一种形状像海豚,但长着锋利牙齿并且会游泳的爬行类动物。

① **fossil** ['fɒs(ə)l; -sɪl] *n.* 化石,僵化的事物、顽固不化的人
② **community** [kə'mju:nətɪ] *n.* 社区、群落、共同体、团体 [communities]
③ **display** [dɪ'spleɪ] *n.* 显示、炫耀;*vt.* 显示、表现、陈列;*vi.* 作炫耀行为
④ **creature** ['kri:tʃə] *n.* 动物、生物、人、创造物
⑤ **pterosaur** ['terəsɔ:] *n.* 翼龙
⑥ **ichthyosaur** ['ɪkθɪəsɔ:] *n.* 鱼龙

Her life changed. The girl grew up strong and healthy and she also found the first complete **plesiosaurus**[1], a large sea reptile that looks like the **legendary**[2] "Loch Ness monster".

Then one day, while she was hunting, there was a huge landslide. It narrowly missed Mary — but killed her dog Tray. She was sad, but had suffered many losses of loved ones in her life. She thanked God for the time she did have with her dog — and then went back to work.

By the time Mary Anning was 27, she had saved enough money to buy a little home with a **shop-front**[3] window where the fossils could be displayed.

She grew up to become one of the most famous fossil-finders in the world. Her little shop is still there. If you visit the UK, you can visit it. It is now called the Lyme Regis Museum, and is well worth a visit.

玛丽的生活彻底改变了。她渐渐长大，身体强壮而健康。她发现了第一个完整的蛇颈龙化石。蛇颈龙是一种大型的海生爬行类动物，看起来就像"尼斯湖水怪"。

有一天，正当玛丽寻找化石的时候，发生了一场山崩。玛丽堪堪幸免于难，但她的小狗"托盘"却不幸遇难。玛丽很伤心，然而，她已经历过太多心爱的人去世的苦难，所以她感谢上帝赐予她这样一段与小狗共度的时光，然后重新投入了工作之中。

27岁时，玛丽·安宁（Mary Anning）攒够了钱，买了一间有橱窗的小房子，在那里陈列她自己发现的化石。

后来，她成为世界上最著名的化石发现家之一。她的小店还在原处，现在改建为林姆·雷吉斯博物馆，非常值得参观。如果你有机会去英国，可以去那里一游。

---

① **plesiosaurus** [ˌplɪsɪə'sɔrəs] *n.* 蛇颈龙（等于 plesiosaur）[plesiosauri]
② **legendary** ['ledʒ(ə)nd(ə)rɪ] *adj.* 传说的、传奇的；*n.* 传说集、圣徒传
　[legendaries]
③ **shop-front** 店面、堂面

THE BOY WHO WENT SEARCHING FOR GIANTS

乔治•居维叶
寻找巨人的男孩

A SIX-YEAR-OLD BOY CALLED GEORGES loved puzzles. But not just the **brainteasers**[1] that you find in newspapers or books.

He loved real life puzzles.

When an **illusionist**[2] came to his town in France and did a series of magic tricks, little Georges Cuvier sat down with paper and pencil and worked out how the man had fooled everyone.

The family lived in the countryside and the boy spent many hours exploring nature with his mother.

And that's where he found the biggest puzzles of all: why was the world like it was? Why were there so many strange and wonderful animals and plants? And why were there so many stories told about giants and dragons and amazing creatures like that?

In Europe, **archeologists**[3] said they had dug up the bones of giant men, who were even taller than the oldest, highest trees in the village.

What happened to the giants? Why had they died out?

As Georges Cuvier grew older, he started to **sketch**[4] flowers and animals, and by the time he was 12, he was an expert naturalist.

一个六岁的男孩名叫乔治，他很喜爱解答谜题，但并不是我们常常在报纸或者书籍中见到的那些智力题。

他喜欢解答现实中的难题。

有一次，一位魔术师来到乔治居住的法国小镇，在他变了一系列的魔术后，年幼的乔治·居维叶（Georges Cuvier）坐在桌子前，用纸和笔推断出了这位魔术师愚弄所有人的技巧。

乔治一家住在乡下，他每天会花好几个小时，和母亲一起去探索大自然的奥秘。

而大自然也带给了乔治一生中最大的困惑：世界为什么是这样的？为什么大自然中有那么多神奇又怪异的动植物？为什么有那么多讲述巨人、龙和类似神奇生物的故事？

欧洲的考古学家声称他们挖到了巨人的骨骼，那些巨人的身高比村庄里年代最悠久、最挺拔的树木还要高。

那么，巨人到底发生了什么？为什么全都灭绝了？

居维叶一天天长大，他开始画花卉和动物素描。12岁时，他已经是一位专业的博物学家了。

① **brainteaser** ['breɪn,tiːzə] n. 测验机敏的难题、令人困惑的问题
② **illusionist** [ɪ'l(j)uːʒ(ə)nɪst] n. 爱幻想的人、幻觉论者、幻觉派的艺术家
③ **archeologist** [,ɑːkɪ'ɒlədʒɪst] n. 考古学家
④ **sketch** [sketʃ] n. 素描，略图，梗概；vt. 画素描或速写；vi. 画素描或速写 [sketches, sketched, sketched, sketching]

Now all this happened in France in the 1700s, when only rich children received serious teaching. A **wealthy**[①] nobleman noticed Georges' skill and paid for him to have a good education.

As an adult, Georges became a professor and decided to **investigate**[②] the giants and other strange animals.

He realized that the fossil bones of the "giants" were not from humans at all. They were the bones of other big animals, such as elephants, and prehistoric creatures, such as **mastodons**[③].

This in itself was surprising, as there were no elephants in that part of Europe.

He found other fossils too, which seemed to belong to animals that were totally unknown!

One of the strangest things that ended up on his work table was a selection of parts of a creature that looked like a large reptile, but had large bat-like wings, and a beak with sharp teeth. (Less than 30 years later, little Mary Anning, who we met in the previous story, would find a related **skeleton**[④] which would go on display as the "Flying Dragon".)

这一切都发生在 18 世纪的法国，那时只有富裕家庭的孩子才能够接受正式的教育。一位富有的贵族注意到了乔治非凡的智慧，出钱资助乔治接受教育。

成年后乔治成了一位教授，他开始调查巨人和其他奇怪的动物。

乔治发现，那些所谓的"巨人"骨骼化石其实根本不来源于人类，它们来源于其他大型动物（比如象）以及史前生物（比如乳齿象）。

这一发现是惊人的，因为当时没有任何大象生活在欧洲的这个区域。

乔治还发现了其他的化石，而那些化石似乎也来源于完全不为人知的动物！

在他的工作台上出现过的最奇怪的一件物品，是一种生物的部分躯体，它看起来像大型爬行类动物，但又长着像蝙蝠一样的翅膀，以及锋利牙齿的喙。（不到 30 年后，年幼的玛丽·安宁，也就是我们在上一个故事中提及的女孩，发现了一具与之类似的骨骼，这具骨骼后来作为"飞龙"进行展出。）

---

① **wealthy** ['welθɪ] adj. 富有的、充分的、丰裕的 [wealthier, wealthiest]
② **investigate** [ɪn'vestɪɡeɪt] v. 调查、研究 [investigated, investigated, investigating]
③ **mastodon** ['mæstədɒn] n. 乳齿象，庞然大物；adj. 巨大的、庞大的
④ **skeleton** ['skelɪt(ə)n] n. 骨架、骨骼、纲要、骨瘦如柴的人；adj. 骨骼的、骨瘦如柴的，概略的

※◦≷◦≶ §◦≷◦≶※

But Georges Cuvier's real **contribution**① to science was an extraordinary idea — if you studied the shape of fossil bones and compared them to the shape of bones of living creatures, you could learn about the past, and how creatures were created or evolved.

And when he put all his findings together, he made a **mind-blowing**② discovery.

We live in a world in which **mammals**③, such as humans, dominate. But before that, there existed an entirely different world, right here, in which a completely different group of creatures, reptile-like animals, were dominant!

Georges Cuvier had discovered the world of the dinosaurs.

※◦≷◦≶ §◦≷◦≶※

Today, this Frenchman is sometimes called "the father of **paleontology**④".

But it's worth remembering that he started down the track to fame walking through the same forests that other people had walked, but being curious enough to ask questions no one had yet asked.

He disproved the tales about giants, but became a "giant of science" himself.

居维叶对于科学真正的贡献①是他杰出的思想——如果你对骨骼化石的形状进行研究，并将它们与现存生物的骨骼形状进行对比，你就能够了解过去，并且了解生物是如何产生和进化的。

当居维叶汇总了自己的研究成果后，他宣布了一项令人惊叹②的发现：

如今我们生活在一个哺乳类动物③（比如人类）主宰的世界中，但在此之前，世界是完全不同的，由一种截然不同的生物——爬行类动物主宰！

乔治·居维叶发现了恐龙的世界。

如今，有人称乔治这位法国人为"古生物学④之父"。

但最值得纪念的是，他走在一条通往盛名的道路上，穿过了其他人同样走过的森林，却能够保持好奇心，思考其他人不曾想过的问题。

他证实了所有关于巨人的传说都是虚构的，而他自己则成了一位"科学的巨人"。

---

① **contribution** [kɒntrɪˈbjuːʃ(ə)n] *n.* 贡献、捐献
② **mind-blowing** 产生幻觉效果的、令人极度兴奋的、给人印象极深的
③ **mammal** [ˈmæm(ə)l] *n.* 哺乳动物
④ **paleontology** [ˌpælɪɒnˈtɒlədʒɪ] 古生物学

LOVE, ROCKS AND THE FIRST DINOSAUR

玛丽·莫兰
爱、岩石和第一只恐龙

STEP C.

MARY'S MOTHER DIED SOON after she was born. The **toddler**[1] was given to a couple who had no children of their own.

This worked out well, because they gave her lots of love, but also educated her, even though in the UK in those days (the early 1800s), only boys were usually allowed to go to school.

She was good at art, and when she was in her twenties, her **adoptive**[2] father gave her some bones (some people thought they were bones of a giant, see the previous story) to draw for a fossil expert he knew.

※※※

By the time she was 27, Mary Morland was fascinated by paleontology, and when a new book came out about rocks and fossils, she bought a copy and took it with her on a train journey.

Now just hold that thought for a moment.

A little distance away lived the fossil expert whom her father knew.

William Buckland was a single professor aged 40. He knew there was a young woman who shared his interests, and he decided to look for her. To **occupy**[3] his mind on the train journey, he took a newly published book on rocks and fossils.

You can guess what happened.

玛丽刚出生不久，她的母亲就去世了。于是，这位还在蹒跚学步的女孩被送给了一对没有孩子的夫妇。

这是个正确的选择，因为这对夫妇很爱玛丽，还给予了她接受教育的机会。在当时的英国（19世纪早期），通常情况下只有男孩才能上学读书。

玛丽擅长艺术，在她20多岁时，她的养父交给她一些骨骼（通过前一则故事你已经了解到，当时的一些人认为那是巨人的骨骼），让她去把它们画下来，这是为他所认识的一位化石专家所做的工作。

到27岁时，玛丽·莫兰（Mary Morland）深深地迷上了古生物学。她买了一本刚出版的有关岩石和化石的新书，并随身带着它，坐上火车去旅行。

现在让我们稍等片刻。

玛丽养父所认识的那位化石专家住得离她不远。

威廉·巴克兰（William Buckland）是一位40岁的单身教授。他知道有一位年轻女子和他有着同样的兴趣，因此打算去和她见一面。为了充实自己在火车上的旅行时光，威廉带上了一本新出版的有关岩石和化石的书。

你可以猜到接下来发生了什么。

······················

① **toddler** [ˈtɒdlə] n. 学步的小孩
② **adoptive** [əˈdɒptɪv] adj. 采用的、有收养关系的
③ **occupy** [ˈɒkjʊpaɪ] vt. 占据、占领，居住，使忙碌 [occupied, occupied, occupying]

The two ended up in the same carriage, holding **identical**[①] books. Love blossomed.

Mary and Will got married and spent a year on honeymoon, visiting famous rock **formations**[②] and fossil experts.

The Bucklands had a great career as paleontologists, and worked well as a team.

For example, one day, explorers saw strange, fossilized **scrape**[③] marks in ancient rocks. What sort of beast could make those marks?

William puzzled over the problem way past midnight. At 2 a.m., he had an idea.

"Mary," he said, "Use flour to make a **paste**[④], and then lay it over the kitchen table." And then he opened the back door and went out into the night. Why? Where was he going?

But she knew her husband well enough to trust that he must have had a brainwave.

He returned with a tortoise from the garden, and placed it on the table. It moved across the floury paste — and made the exact same marks. They now knew the marks were the fossilized tracks of an ancient tortoise.

威廉和玛丽带着同样的书，在同一节车厢里相逢了。

他们之间产生了爱情的火花，很快就结婚了。他们花了一年的时间度蜜月，同时到处拜访著名的岩层与化石专家。

巴克兰一家都是古生物学家，并且作为一个团队，工作很有成效。

比如，有一天，探险家们在古岩层上看到了石化的奇怪刮痕。什么类型的野兽能够产生这种刮痕呢？

威廉整晚都被这个问题所困扰，直到午夜过后，凌晨两点时，他想出了一个办法。

"玛丽，"他说，"用面粉做一个面团，把它放在厨房的桌子上。"然后他打开房间后门，走进了夜幕中。怎么回事？他要到哪里去？

好在玛丽很了解她的丈夫，相信他一定是产生了灵感。

威廉从花园中带回了一只乌龟，把它放在桌上。乌龟从面团上爬过，留下了和岩石上的刮痕相同的痕迹。他们意识到，那些石化的刮痕是由古代的乌龟造成的。

---

① **identical** [aɪˈdentɪk(ə)l] *adj.* 同一的、完全相同的；*n.* 完全相同的事物
② **formation** [fɔːˈmeɪʃ(ə)n] *n.* 形成、构造，编队
③ **scrape** [skreɪp] *n.* 刮掉、擦痕，困境，刮擦声。*vt.* 刮、擦伤，挖成。*vi.* 刮掉、刮出刺耳声 [scraped, scraped, scraping]
④ **paste** [peɪst] *vt.* 张贴、裱糊、用糨糊粘；*n.* 面团、膏、糊状物、糨糊 [pasted, pasted, pasting]

. When William was an old man, he used his knowledge of rocks to play a final joke. He told the **gravedigger**[1] that he wanted to be buried in a certain place.

After his death, they discovered that the spot had just a few inches of soil, below which was a huge **slab**[2] of **Jurassic**[3] rock. It was impossible to dig there.

But they were determined to follow his wishes. They used explosives to make a hole big enough for the grave.

Mary died the following year.

If you look up the name of the very first dinosaur to be given a scientific name, you'll find **Megalosaurus bucklandii**[4]. Can you see what's hidden in the second part of that name? Yes, it's the family name of William and Mary Buckland.

威廉垂垂老矣，他运用自己了解的岩石知识，开了人生中最后一个玩笑。他告诉替他挖墓的人，自己想被埋葬在某一个特定的地方。

在他去世后，挖墓人发现他选择的埋葬地点的泥土只有几英寸厚，土下面是一大块侏罗纪时期的岩石。在那里挖个墓的可能性极低。

但是他们决定完成威廉的遗愿。他们用炸药在那里炸开了一个大洞，建造坟墓。

威廉去世后的第二年，玛丽也去世了。

如果你去查阅第一只拥有学名的恐龙，你会发现它叫"Megalosaurus bucklandii"（巴氏斑龙）。你发现第二个单词隐藏着的内容了吗？是的，那是威廉·巴克兰和玛丽·巴克兰两人的姓。

---

① **gravedigger** [ˈgreɪvdɪgə] *n.* 挖墓者、埋葬虫
② **slab** [slæb] *n.* 厚板、平板、混凝土路面、厚片；*vt.* 把……分成厚片、用石板铺
　[slabbed, slabbed, slabbing]
③ **Jurassic** [dʒuˈræsik] *adj.* 侏罗系的、侏罗纪的；*n.* 侏罗纪
④ **Megalosaurus bucklandii** 巴氏斑龙

THE BUG BOY SOLVES A HUGE MYSTERY

路易斯·阿加西
揭开巨大谜团的昆虫男孩

THE BUG BOY WAS PUZZLED. His family had no money, so his playground was the area of woods and fields around his **humble**[1] home in Switzerland.

Yet the things he found outdoors did not make sense.

Rocks from one mountain were found on top of another. Fish fossils were discovered far away from any sea. And natural features like hills and cliffs were often **striped**[2] with straight lines that seemed to point to something. But what?

The boy's name was Louis Agassiz, and he was 10 years old. We call him the bug boy because he often took creatures home with him. He would keep **caterpillars**[3] in jars and watch carefully to see how they turned into butterflies.

Then his parents gave him some big news. They had saved enough money to send him to school for the first time — but the school was far away.

He was sad to leave them, but knew that this was an **opportunity**[4] he should take. He also missed his brother, Auguste, who was not interested in bugs, but was fascinated by machines — especially tiny ones such as the insides of watches.

As Louis Agassiz grew into a young teenager, he did not lose his love of nature, and soon had a whole, live tree into the room where he lived — and made sure that there were birds and bugs in the tree, so he could study them.

昆虫男孩很烦恼。他住在瑞士，家庭并不富裕，所以只能在自己家简陋房子旁的树林中和田野上玩耍。

然而在户外发现的东西让他感觉很困惑。

一座山脉上的岩石在另一座山峰的山顶上被发现了。鱼类的化石在远离海洋的地方被发现了。丘陵和悬崖这些自然地貌总带有直线条纹，好像在说明着什么。但究竟是什么呢？

这个 10 岁的男孩名叫路易斯·阿加西（Louis Agassiz）。我们称他为"昆虫男孩"，因为他常常把一些昆虫带回家。他会把毛毛虫装在罐子里，认真地观察它们是如何变成蝴蝶的。

不久，他的父母告诉了他一个好消息。他们终于攒够了钱，可以送他去学校读书了——但是学校很远。

因为要离开父母，路易斯感到很难过，但他知道他必须抓住这个机会。他也很想念哥哥奥古斯都（Auguste）。哥哥对昆虫不感兴趣，但很喜欢研究机械设备——尤其是小型的机械，比如说手表的内部构造。

长成一名少年后，路易斯·阿加西仍然热爱着大自然，并且在自己的房间里种了一整棵树——确保树上生活着鸟儿和昆虫，以便自己开展研究。

① **humble** ['hʌmbl] *adj.* 谦逊的，简陋的，（级别或地位）低下的、不大的；*vt.* 使谦恭，轻松打败（尤指强大的对手）、低声下气
② **stripe** [straɪp] *n.* 条纹、斑纹，种类；*vt.* 加条纹于……[striped, striped, striping]
③ **caterpillar** ['kætəpɪlə] *n.* 毛虫、履带车；*adj.* 有履带装置的
④ **opportunity** [ˌɒpə'tjuːnətɪ] *n.* 时机、机会 [opportunities]

I don't think most modern children would like a tree full of birds and bugs in their bedroom!

When he was fifteen, his parents told him that he had to stop studying and get a job — that was the normal age to finish education in those days, the 1820s.

But the boy begged to be allowed to go on studying, and the parents, who were a preacher and his wife, saved up more money and let him carry on.

Louis Agassiz went to study mountains and built himself a **hut**[1] on top of a **glacier**[2] — a river of ice.

There he studied the way that glaciers moved rocks and fossils around, and he and his **colleagues**[3] found the answer to a huge puzzle. An unimaginably big glacier, an ice **sheet**[4], must have covered many countries in the past. It would have covered Britain and most of Europe. And that's why so many things had moved, with rocks and bones from one area found in other areas, miles away.

The bug boy had discovered the **Ice Age**[5].

Many years later, other scientists investigated this idea, and found that the theory was right. More than a quarter of the landmasses of the planet had been covered with a huge sheet of ice, 20,000 years ago.

我想，现代社会中大多数的孩子不会乐意自己的卧室里有一棵满是鸟儿和昆虫的大树的！

当路易斯 15 岁时，父母告诉他不能再上学了，他得去找一份工作——在 19 世纪 20 年代，15 岁是结束教育的正常年龄。

但是阿加西恳求父母让他继续学业，最终，做牧师的父亲以及母亲又攒了些钱，供他继续读书。

路易斯·阿加西学习了关于山脉的知识，并在一条冰川上建造了一间屋子。

在那里，路易斯研究让岩石和化石四处移动的冰川，他和同事找到了一个巨大谜团的答案。在远古，必定有一片无比巨大的冰盖覆盖住了许多国家，包括英国和欧洲的大部分地区。这就是为什么如此众多的物体会移动的原因，某个区域的岩石和骨骼会在相隔数千米远的另一个区域被发现。

这个昆虫男孩确认（地质史上）存在过冰期。

多年以后，其他的科学家针对这个理论开展调查研究，发现它是正确的。两万年前，地球上超过四分之一的大陆都被一大块冰盖覆盖着。

① **hut** [hʌt] *n.* 小屋、临时营房；*vt.* 使住在小屋中、驻扎；*vi.* 住在小屋中、驻扎 [hutted, hutted, hutting]
② **glacier** ['glæsɪə; 'gleɪsɪə] *n.* 冰河、冰川
③ **colleague** ['kɒliːɡ] *n.* 同事、同僚 [colleagues]
④ **sheet** [ʃiːt] *n.* 薄片、张、薄板、床单；*adj.* 片状的
⑤ **Ice Age** 冰期、冰河时代

Louis became famous. But so did his brother, in a different way. Sometimes you might see **advertisements**[1] for a famous watch brand called Longines. That's the company of the bug-boy's brother.

Their parents, in their little church in the hills, must have been proud of both of them.

路易斯声名大噪，而他的哥哥也以另一种方式闻名于世。你可能看到过一个著名手表品牌——浪琴的广告，这款手表就出自这个昆虫男孩哥哥的公司。

　　他们居住在山上小教堂里的父母，一定为自己的两个儿子感到骄傲吧！

---

① **advertisement** [əd'vɜːtɪsmənt] *n.* 广告、宣传

THE WOMAN WHO SAW DEEP INTO THE EARTH

英奇·莱曼
了解地球深处的女子

LOTS OF PEOPLE LIKE interesting stones and **pebbles**[1], but Inge loved extremely big rocks: she loved mountains.

One day when she was in her mid-teens she was sitting on the sofa with her mother and sister on a Sunday morning.

She felt the ground beneath her feet **tremble**[2] and then everything shook — the seats, the walls, and even the ceiling. The lamp above her head swung from side to side.

Her father rushed into the room. "It was an earthquake," he said.

And so, Inge Lehmann, a girl born in 1888 in Denmark, became interested in the biggest rock of all: the planet Earth, third rock from the sun.

Twenty years after experiencing that earthquake, she was a **seismologist**[3].

That means she was an expert in measuring movements under the ground — the shaking that **accompanies**[4] earthquakes, but also happens in less **disruptive**[5] ways at other times.

Inge and her colleagues realized that if you collected a lot of detailed records about earthquakes you could work out a surprisingly large amount of information about what was deep inside the Earth — deeper than any explorer could reach.

很多人喜欢好看的小石子和鹅卵石，但是英奇却喜欢巨大的岩石——她喜欢高山。

在她十五六岁时，一个周日的早晨，她和母亲、姐姐一起坐在沙发上。

她突然感到脚下的地面开始震动，接着所有的东西——椅子、墙壁甚至天花板都开始摇晃起来。头顶上的吊灯不断地来回摆动。

她的父亲冲进了房间，喊道："地震了！"

从此以后，这位出生于1888年的丹麦女孩——英奇·莱曼（Inge Lehmann）就开始对世界上最大的一块岩石，也是太阳系中距离太阳第三远的行星——地球感兴趣了。

在经历了这场地震的20年后，她成为一名地震学家。

也就是说，她是一位测量地球内部运动的专家。地球内部运动有时伴随着地震，但有时破坏力也不大。

英奇和同事发现，如果收集大量的有关地震的详细记录，然后进行分析，便能发现地球深处大量的信息——没有任何探险家能够到达那个深度。

① **pebble** [ˈpeb(ə)l] n. 卵石、水晶透镜；vt. 用卵石铺 [pebbled, pebbled, pebbling]
② **tremble** [ˈtremb(ə)l] vi. 发抖、战栗、焦虑、摇晃；vt. 使挥动、用颤抖的声音说出 [trembled, trembled, trembling]
③ **seismologist** [saizˈmɒlədʒist, sais-] n. 地震学家
④ **accompany** [əˈkʌmpəni] vt. 陪伴、伴随、伴奏；vi. 伴奏、伴唱 [accompanied, accompanied, accompanying]
⑤ **disruptive** [disˈrʌptiv] adj. 破坏的、分裂性的、制造混乱的

She spent months studying the data and realized that 250 kilometers under our feet, something changed. The Earth had a different **texture**[1] that far down.

Scientists today call this the **Lehmann Discontinuity**[2], naming it after its discoverer.

But then Inge Lehmann found something even more interesting. Until then, scientists had believed that the center of the Earth was a huge **molten**[3] ball.

She studied the way that trembles and shakes ran through the planet and came to a different conclusion. The core of the planet had two sections. The outer core was molten, like a superheated liquid, but right at the center of the world, there was an incredibly hot, solid ball of metal. Scientists checked her results and realized that they explained the data perfectly. People were amazed that a woman working in an office on the surface of the world could detect what was in the planet's center!

When Inge was an old woman, she spent her summers quietly in a **cottage**[4] away from the city. Once a visitor came to see her — and was amazed to find that Inge had chosen a room at the top of the house for herself, and climbed up a **ladder**[5] every night to get there.

❦❦❦

英奇花了好几个月研究这些数据,并发现在地表之下 250 千米深处,有一些物质正在发生变化。地球内部的结构与外界是完全不同的。

因为这是莱曼的发现,如今的科学家将其称为莱曼不连续面。

但很快,英奇·莱曼发现了一些更有趣的情况。在那之前,科学家们都认为地球中心是一颗巨大的呈熔融态的圆球。

英奇对贯穿地球的震动和摇晃路线进行了研究,得出了一个完全不同的结论:地球的内核分为两个部分。地核的外部是熔融态的,就像一团过热的液体;但在地核中心,是一块球状的温度极高的固体金属。科学家验证了她的结论,发现它们完美地解释了那些地震数据。当时的人们很惊讶,在位于地表的办公室里工作的女子,竟然能够侦测到地球中心的情况!

❦❦❦

步入暮年后,英奇经常在远离城市的一座村舍中安静地度过夏天。有一次,一个人来拜访她,惊讶地发现她挑选了一个屋顶的房间居住,每个晚上都要借助梯子才能爬上去!

---

① **texture** ['tekstʃə] n. 质地、纹理,结构,本质、实质 [textured, textured, texturing]
② **Lehmann Discontinuity** 莱曼不连续面,是指在地球的地幔中地震波 P 波和 S 波突然加速的区域,该区域一般在 220±30 千米深处
③ **melt** [melt] vi. 熔化、溶解;vt. 使融化、使熔化、使软化、使感动;n. 熔化、熔化物 [melted, melted 或 molten,melting]
④ **cottage** ['kɒtɪdʒ] n. 小屋、村舍、(农舍式的)小别墅
⑤ **ladder** ['lædə] n. 阶梯、途径,梯状物;vt. 在……上装设梯子

Even at the age of 70, mountain-lover Inge Lehmann still loved climbing.

She died at the age of 104 in 1993.

If one hot day you can become powerfully aware that the sun is a **fiery**[3] ball above your head, take a moment to remember the Danish scientist who discovered that there is another fiery hot ball beneath our feet.

即使 70 岁了，爬山运动爱好者英奇·莱曼仍然热衷于登山。

1993 年，英奇离开了人世，享年 104 岁。

如果在某个炎热的夏天，你强烈地感受到，头顶上的太阳是一颗炙热的球体，请花点时间缅怀一下这位丹麦的科学家——英奇，是她发现我们脚下还存在着另一颗炙热的球体。

③ fiery ['faɪərɪ] adj. 热烈的、炽烈的，暴躁的、燃烧般的 [fierier, fieriest]

THE BOY WHO DECODED THE DANCE OF THE STARS

杰里迈亚·霍罗克斯
破译星星舞蹈的男孩

JEREMIAH LOVED THE STARS, but he was too young and too poor to be an **astronomer**①.

He was the child of a poor family in the UK a long time ago, in the early 1600s.

While other children played, Jeremiah Horrocks saved his energy until the evening, when he could watch the stars starting to **twinkle**② in the deep blue evening sky.

The way they "danced" in different directions and at different speeds as they moved across the sky might be a **code**③ which could reveal secrets about the galaxy, he believed.

When he was 13, Jeremiah, who was very bright, went to university, where he learned from astronomers and used their **telescopes**④.

But before he could graduate, his family ran out of money, and he had to return home.

He was sad at first, but then had an idea. His father worked for a watchmaker. He knew how to do three things: shape metal, form circles of glass, and make very **precise**⑤ **instruments**⑥.

These were the exact three things you needed to make a telescope!

By the time he was in his late teens, Jeremiah was working to earn money during the day (he was a **trainee**⑦ church pastor and a private tutor), and he was working with his family members to make his own telescope during the evenings.

杰里迈亚热爱星空，但他年龄太小，家里太穷，他不可能成为一名天文学家。

17世纪早期，他出生于英国的一个贫困家庭。

当（白天）其他孩子玩耍时，杰里迈亚·霍罗克斯（Jeremiah Horrocks）则一直在养精蓄锐，以便晚上有精力观察在深蓝色的夜空中闪烁的星星。

他相信，星星们穿越长空时，是在以不同的速度、向不同的方向"跳舞"，它们"跳舞"的方式也许能揭开银河系的秘密。

杰里迈亚非常聪明，他13岁就上了大学，跟随着天文学家学习，使用他们的望远镜。

但还没毕业，他家里就没钱再供他读书了，他不得不辍学回家。

他一开始很伤心，但很快想出了一个办法。他的父亲为一位钟表匠工作，知道如何制作三件东西：金属架、圆形玻璃和精密的设备。

这三件东西就是制作一架望远镜所必需的！

杰里迈亚十八九岁时，他白天赚钱（他是一所教堂的实习牧师，还做着一份私人家教），晚上和家人一起制作望远镜。

---

① **astronomer** [əˈstrɒnəmə] *n.* 天文学家
② **twinkle** [ˈtwɪŋk(ə)l] *vi.* 闪烁、发亮；*vt.* 使闪耀、闪耀 [twinkled, twinkled, twinkling]
③ **code** [kəʊd] *n.* 代码、密码、编码、法典
④ **telescope** [ˈtelɪskəʊp] *n.* 望远镜、缩叠式旅行袋。
⑤ **precise** [prɪˈsaɪs] *adj.* 精确的、明确的、严格的 [more precise, most precise]
⑥ **instrument** [ˈɪnstrʊm(ə)nt] *n.* 仪器、工具、乐器、器械
⑦ **trainee** [treɪˈniː] *n.* 练习生、实习生、受训者，新兵，训练中的动物

One day, when he was 19 or 20, his observations of star movements gave him an idea.

Although the sun appeared to rise in the East and move across the sky to the West, he was **convinced**① that it was actually a huge distance away, much further than the moon, hundreds of thousands of miles or kilometers from the Earth.

And he realized that he could actually prove it, if he was right about the way the lights in the heavens continued on their dances.

On one particular day soon, according to his calculations, the planet **Venus**② would come in between the Earth and the Sun, far out in space.

This would be proof that the sun was not in the sky, as it seemed to be, but an unimaginably large distance away.

That day, he got up at sunrise. He knew he should not look directly at the sun, so he set up his telescope to **project**③ an image of the sun onto a piece of paper.

And he watched and waited.

It was disappointing. He saw nothing interesting, although he watched for hours.

In the afternoon, clouds appeared and both he and the sky became **gloomy**④.

But then, at 3.15 p.m., the clouds parted.

在霍罗克斯大概 19 或 20 岁的某一天，他从观察星轨中得到了一点启示。

太阳看起来是从东方升起，在天空中移动，然后到西方落下，但霍罗克斯认为，它距离我们很远，比地球和月球之间几十万千米的距离还要远。

而且他意识到，如果自己关于星星在天空中移动轨迹的看法是正确的，自己应该可以证明。

很快，在一个特殊的日子里，根据霍罗克斯的计算，遥远外太空中的金星将移动到太阳和地球之间。

这将是太阳不在我们附近天空之中的证据，尽管看起来太阳就在那里，但其实它在难以想象的遥远距离外。

那天，霍罗克斯在日出时就起床了。他知道不可以直视太阳，因此他架起望远镜，利用它在一张纸上投射太阳的影像。

然后他等待着、观察着。

令人失望的是，尽管他观察了好几个小时，却没有看到任何有趣的现象。

下午的时候，天空中出现了云层，天色变得阴暗起来，他的心情也随之变得沮丧起来。

但在下午 3 点 15 分时，云层散开了。

---

① **convince** [kən'vɪns] *v.* 使确信、说服
② **Venus** ['viːnəs] *n.* 金星、维纳斯（爱与美的女神）
③ **project** [prə'dʒekt; 'prɒdʒekt] *vi.* 设计、计划、表达、投射；*vt.* 设计、计划、发射、放映；*n.* 工程、计划、事业
④ **gloomy** ['gluːmɪ] *adj.* 黑暗的、沮丧的、阴郁的 [gloomier, gloomiest]

His telescope showed an amazing sight! He could see a dot crossing a circle.

He knew exactly what it was. In his head, he could visualize a huge planet as a small, round, dark **silhouette**[①] passing in front of a massive burning fire-golden **orb**[②].

This proved the sun was tens of millions of miles away, further than Venus.

He wrote down his findings — partly in poetry — and then sent them to London, to the **Royal Society**[③], the world's top science organization.

But this story has a sad ending. In those days, medical science was undeveloped, and people who got sick often died. Jeremiah Horrocks became ill and died at the age of 22.

Years later, people discovered his letter and realized that he was one of the greatest scientists in the country, even though he was just a child when he did most of his work.

In 2012, scientists using special hi-tech cameras in space watched, for the first time, Venus crossing in front of the sun in clear detail (and you can watch it yourself on the Internet: look up "**transit**[④] of Venus").

Humanity finally saw what young Jeremiah had seen in his head 400 years earlier!

他的望远镜显示,天空中出现了一道惊人的景象!霍罗克斯看到一个圆点正在穿过一个圆形物体。

对此现象他清楚万分。在他的脑海里,他看到一颗巨大的行星,如同一个小小的黑色圆形轮廓,正从另一颗更大的熊熊燃烧的金色天体前穿过。

这个现象证明了,太阳离我们起码有数千万千米远,比金星还远得多!

他将自己的发现记录下来(部分以诗歌的形式),并寄给了世界顶级科学机构——位于伦敦的英国皇家学会。

但是这个故事的结局是令人悲伤的。在那时,医学并不发达,得病的人多半会死去。杰里迈亚·霍罗克斯生病了,22 岁就离开了人世。

很多年后,人们发现了他写的信,意识到他是那个国家最伟大的科学家之一,虽然他的工作大部分都是在孩提时期完成的。

2012 年,科学家利用太空中一台特制的高科技相机,第一次观察到了金星从太阳表面穿过的细节(你可以自己在网上搜索"金星凌日"观看)。

最终,人类目睹了 400 年前年轻的霍罗克斯头脑中发生的场景!

---

① **silhouette** [ˌsɪluˈet] *n.* 轮廓、剪影;*vt.* 使……照出影子来、使……仅仅显出轮廓 [silhouetted, silhouetted, silhouetting]
② **orb** [ɔːb] *n.* 球、天体、圆形物;*vt.* 弄圆、围着;*vi.* 沿轨道运行
③ **Royal Society**(英)皇家学会
④ **transit** [ˈtrænsɪt; ˈtrɑːns-; -nz-] *n.* 运输、经过;*vt.* 运送;*vi.* 经过 [transited, transited, transiting]

THE POET-SCIENTIST WHO DETECTED AN EARTHQUAKE

张衡
感测地震的诗人兼科学家

THE FUTURE LOOKED BAD for a boy called Zhang Heng, aged ten. The family did not have much money, and then his father died.

Even worse, Heng was only really good at one thing: writing poems. What use was that? He was a **bookworm**[①], not like his grandfather, who was an army **commander**[②]. The family struggled to survive.

When Zhang Heng was 16 years old, in the year 95 AD, he left his hometown of Xi'e in Nanyang, Henan province, China, and started to travel to the big city nearby, to see if he could get a job.

On his way, he stopped at a **hot spring**[③] and wrote a poem about it.

Then he arrived in town. The good thing was that people in power in the big city remembered his family's past achievements, and agreed to see him. It turned out that they were in need of writers — so he was given a post as a **Master of Documents**[④] for the officials in the government.

Being a bookworm can be a good thing.

His poem about the hot springs became famous.

One day, when Zhang Heng was 30, he stared up at the night sky.

That's the sort of thing most poets do. But instead of just writing a poem about it, he started to notice things.

有一个名叫张衡的 10 岁男孩,他的未来看起来很不乐观。他的家境并不富裕,父亲又去世了。

更糟糕的是,张衡只擅长做一件事:写诗。那有什么用呢?他是个书呆子,而不像他的祖父一样是位军事指挥家。这个家庭正在夹缝中求生存。

公元 95 年,当张衡 16 岁时,他离开了家乡——中国河南省南阳的西鄂,准备去附近的大城市寻找一份工作。

在途中,他在一个温泉附近停了下来,写了一首关于它的诗。

他到了城里。对他来说有个好消息是,城里的权贵还记得他们家族曾经的辉煌,同意接见他。结果,由于他们需要擅长写作的人,张衡得到了一个"主簿"的职位,掌管文书工作,为政府官员服务。

当一个书呆子也可能是件好事。

他那首关于温泉的诗开始流行起来。

30 岁时,有一天,他抬头仰望夜空。

这是大多数诗人都会做的事,但张衡不是为了写一首关于天空的诗,他开始观察天空。

① **bookworm** [ˈbʊkwɜːm] *n.* 书呆子、蠹鱼、蛀书虫
② **commander** [kəˈmɑːndə] *n.* 指挥官、司令官
③ **hot spring** 温泉
④ **Master of Document**(中国古代官名)主簿

The moon had two sides, a light side that we always saw, and a dark side that was always invisible. And he realized that it was the sun shining on the moon that caused it to seem to change shape. In reality, it didn't change shape at all.

He noticed **constellations**① of stars, and separate stars which seemed to be on their own. He decided to make a star map.

These sort of activities seem normal to us today — but in those days, almost 2,000 years ago — he was one of the first of his kind.

And remember, he had no telescope or **binoculars**②, or even glasses. He just waited until night and then gazed up at the sky.

Zhang Heng **catalogued**③ more than 2,500 stars, and his observations made him one of the first great astronomers. Some of his star maps still survive today. His work was continued almost 2,000 years later by a young woman, as we will learn later in this book.

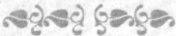

Having fallen in love with science, Zhang Heng did other things too. He is said to have invented a **seismometer**④, which is a machine to detect earthquakes.

One day, the device **trembled**⑤, and indicated a particular direction.

月球有两面，一面是我们总能看到的亮处，另一面是我们永远也看不到的暗处。他意识到，我们看到月球形状在不断"改变"，其实是太阳光照射月球的不同地方所导致的。事实上，月球形状根本没有改变。

他注意到了由恒星构成的星座，并将看似独立的星星一个个区分开来。他决定绘制一张星图。

这种行为在当今看起来很正常，但在那时——大约 2000 年前，他是第一批那么做的人之一。

而且要知道，当时他没有望远镜，甚至连眼镜都没有。他只是静静地等待夜幕降临，然后仰望天空。

张衡的星图编录了 2500 多颗星星，他的这一观察使他成为早期第一批伟大的天文学家之一。

他的一些星图至今仍然保存完好。大约 2000 年后，一名年轻女子将他的工作延续了下去，我们会在本书的后面讲到这名女子的故事。

张衡深深地爱上了科学，他还做了一些其他的事。据说他发明了用来感测地震的地动仪。

有一天，这个装置震动了，并指示了一个特定方位。

① **constellation** [ˌkɒnstəˈleɪʃ(ə)n] *n.* 星座、星群
② **binocular** [bɪˈnɒkjʊlə] *adj.* 双眼的、双目并用的；*n.* 双筒望远镜。
③ **catalogue** [ˈkæt(ə)lɒɡ] *n.* 目录、大学情况一览；*vt.* 把……编入目录 [catalogued, catalogued, cataloguing]
④ **seismometer** [saɪzˈmɒmɪtə] *n.* 地震仪、地震检波器
⑤ **tremble** [ˈtremb(ə)l] *n.* 颤抖、战栗、摇晃；*vi.* 发抖、战栗；*vt.* 使挥动、用颤抖的声音说出 [trembled, trembled, trembling]

"Look," he told the other nobles. "It says there has just been an earthquake to the northwest."

But had that really happened? The matter was discussed, and citizens agreed that none of them had felt any kind of **tremor**[①].

Just when everyone was starting to think he might be a bit crazy, a rider arrived, breathless, saying that there had been an earthquake 400 kilometers to the northwest.

There is not enough information about his device to know for sure how it works, but there is enough detail given about it to intrigue people. So many inventors have tried to recreate his seismograph machine, none successfully yet.

Zhang Heng soon became a powerful nobleman, and he attracted enemies who said bad things about him to the emperor.

He responded in a way that only he could. To set the record straight, he wrote a poem.

"看，"他对其他官员说，"地动仪显示，西北方刚刚发生了一次地震。"

但真的发生地震了吗？大家讨论起这个问题，居民表示他们没有感受到任何震动。

正当每个人都开始觉得张衡可能精神不太正常的时候，一名骑手气喘吁吁地赶来了，告诉大家说400千米远的西北方刚刚发生了一场地震。

虽然（现在）没有足够的信息显示这个地动仪是如何工作的，但关于它的信息足够使人们感到好奇，所以很多发明家努力想重造张衡的地动仪，不过没有人成功。

张衡很快成为一名有权势的贵族，但遭到了一些坏人的诬陷，他们向皇帝说张衡的坏话。

张衡以他独有的方式作出回应——写诗，以此澄清事实真相。

---

① **tremor** ['tremə] *n.* 震颤、颤动

THE FARM BOY WHO SAW THE GALAXIES FLYING AWAY

维斯托·斯里弗
看到星系飞移的农场男孩

GETTING UP EARLY CAN BE HARD. But what if you worked on a farm, and had to get up so early that it was always still dark?

A boy called Vesto Slipher had to do that. But he didn't mind.

He loved the night sky — and began to feel that his future might be up there, in the stars. It was 1875 in the USA, and the night sky was huge and black and **glittery**[1], with no airplanes or pollution. And that meant that you could see all sorts of things above you: not just the moon and stars, but the twinkling **Milky Way**[2] and magical distant star clouds.

It was a good thing he had an interest, because he was one of 11 children, so he didn't get much attention from his parents.

He worked hard and studied hard, and soon got into a university to study astronomy and engineering.

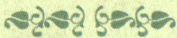

In 1901, his professor asked a rich and famous local astronomer, Percival Lowell, to give the hardworking young man a job at his observatory.

Lowell was a busy man, and so he was not very **enthusiastic**[3] about managing a youngster. But he said he would give a "short-term" contract to the young man, so that the lad could get a little work experience.

But the pair turned into a good team. Slipher was quiet and shy, so he was **unobtrusive**[4] — which means he preferred to work quietly in the background. But he also worked very hard, producing a lot of interesting results.

早早起床是一件困难的事，但如果你在农场工作，每天不得不在天还没亮的时候就起床，该怎么办呢？

一个名叫维斯托·斯里弗（Vesto Slipher）的男孩就是这样，但是他并不在意这些。

他热爱着夜空——他觉得他的未来可能就在星空中。那是1875年的美国，黑沉沉的夜空一望无际，星星在闪烁，没有飞机和污染。这意味着你能看到天上所有的东西：不仅仅是月亮和星星，还有闪烁着的银河和神奇遥远的星云。

斯里弗有这样的一个兴趣是件好事，因为他们家有11个孩子，他不可能得到父母太多的关注。

他努力工作、努力学习，很快进入了大学，学习天文学和工程学。

✦✦✦

1901年，斯里弗的教授请求当地富有的著名天文学家帕西瓦尔·洛威尔（Percival Lowell），在他的天文台给这位勤奋的年轻人安排一份工作。

洛威尔很忙，所以他对给这个年轻人安排一份工作并没有太大的热情，但他回复教授说，他会给这个年轻人一份"短期"合同，这样这个年轻人就可以获得一些工作经验。

这两个人最终成了一对好搭档。斯里弗安静、腼腆，谦虚而不喜欢引人注目——这意味着他更喜欢在幕后默默工作。不过，他工作非常努力，得出了很多有趣的结果。

① **glittery** [ˈɡlɪtəri] *adj.* 闪烁的、闪光的
② **Milky Way** 银河、银河系
③ **enthusiastic** [ɪnˌθjuːziˈæstɪk; en-] *adj.* 热情的、热心的、狂热的 [more enthusiastic, most enthusiastic]
④ **unobtrusive** [ˌʌnəbˈtruːsɪv] *adj.* 不唐突的、谦虚的、不引人注目的

In contrast, Lowell was **flamboyant**[1] and loved to be the center of attention, explaining to the press and public what the results that Slipher collected meant.

The "short-term" contract turned into **partnership**[2] which lasted more than 50 years!

One day, Lowell told Vesto Slipher to do a difficult job: to take pictures of distant star clouds, or **nebulae**[3] (huge clouds of space dust), and analyze the light that came from them, using equipment to break the white light into a rainbow of colors, and recording the differences, if any.

Vesto spent weeks working on this, and noticed something odd — some star clouds had a blue **blur**[4], and others had a red blur.

He knew from his science studies what this meant. Things looked blue if they were speeding towards you and red if they were speeding away from you.

He reported to his boss that the distant star clouds were actually galaxies moving at high speed — up to 1,000 kilometers a second, faster than the fastest jet aircraft!

This was the moment when humanity discovered the truth about the universe. It looked still — but it was really a hyper-active place, with everything moving.

与之相反，洛威尔惹人注目、喜欢得到众人的关注，他向媒体和公众解释斯里弗的研究结果。

"短期"合同变成了长期合作，他们的合作持续了50多年！

✦✦✦

有一天，洛威尔交给斯里弗一项艰巨的工作：拍摄遥远的星云或星系（由太空星尘组成的巨大云状物）的照片，分析它们发出的光线，并利用仪器把白光分解为七色。如果发现有任何差异，随时记录下来。

斯里弗花了好几个星期开展工作，他注意到了一些奇怪的现象——一些星云呈现模糊的蓝色，而另一些则呈现模糊的红色。

根据自己的科学研究他马上明白这意味着什么。当物体快速移动靠近你时，它看起来是蓝色的；当物体快速移动远离你时，它看起来是红色的。

他向老板汇报说，遥远的星云其实是快速移动的星系——它们的速度最高可以达到每秒 1000 千米。比最快的喷气式飞机还要快！

这是人类发现宇宙奥秘的伟大时刻！宇宙看起来是静止的，但其实是一个高度活跃的空间，其中所有的物体都在移动。

---

① **flamboyant** [flæm'bɔɪənt] *adj.* 艳丽的、火焰似的、炫耀的
② **partnership** ['pɑːtnəʃɪp] *n.* 合伙、合伙企业、合作关系、合伙契约
③ **nebulae** ['nɛbjʊli] *n.* 星云
④ **blur** [blɜː] *n.* 污迹、模糊不清的事物；*vt.* 涂污、使……模糊不清、使暗淡、玷污；*vi.* 沾上污迹、变模糊 [blurred, blurred, blurring]

And what's more, we were in just one galaxy, out of many hundreds of thousands of galaxies, all **zooming**[①] around at unimaginable speeds.

The finding eventually led to scientists making lots of other discoveries, such as the fact that the universe was expanding, that it was very old, and that it might have come from a **Big Bang**[②], and so on.

But all this came from the simplest of beginnings: a boy on a farm, looking up at the night sky and wanting to **unravel**[③] the mysteries above him.

而且，我们只是身处其中一个星系中。在这个星系之外，宇宙中还存在着数不清的以令人难以想象的速度移动着的星系。

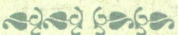

这一发现引导科学家们作出了许多其他的新发现，例如，宇宙一直都在膨胀，宇宙的历史很悠久，宇宙可能起源于一场大爆炸，等等。

然而，所有这一切都源于一个最简单的开头：一位仰望夜空、想要揭开宇宙奥秘的农场男孩。

① **zoom** [zuːm] *n.* 急速上升、嗡嗡声、变焦摄影；*vi.* 急速上升、摄像机移动
② **Big Bang** *n.* 宇宙大爆炸、创世大爆炸
③ **unravel** [ʌnˈrævl] *vt.* 解开、阐明、解决、拆散；*vi.* 解决、散开 [unraveled 或 unravelled, unraveled 或 unravelled, unraveling 或 unravelling]

THE GIRL WHO NAMED THE STARS IN THE SKY

安妮·强普·坎农
为星星命名的女孩

HAVE YOU EVER LOOKED up at the sky on a dark night and seen stars coming into focus over your head?

If you are away from city lights, sometimes you can see hundreds, or even thousands of stars. It's an **entrancing**[1] sight.

Now, there was one particular child who had this experience, and made an amazing decision early in her life: she wanted to identify every single star in the sky, however long it took!

But there was one problem. She was a girl.

In those days, the late 1800s, many jobs were reserved for men only — and particularly jobs which involved mathematics and science.

So this young lady, whose name was Annie Jump Cannon, joined an observatory — a building with telescopes with which people studied the night sky.

Because she was a girl, the men told her that she could never be promoted above the rank of "assistant". The "proper" jobs were **reserved**[2] for men. This seems shocking to us now, but it was normal in those days, not just in the USA where she lived, but around the world.

The work turned out to be really hard. She needed to create a system that divided the entire night sky into sections, and find a way to write down the location of each **pinpoint**[3] of light.

你是否曾经在黑夜里仰望天空，认真观察头顶上令人注目的星星？

如果远离城市的灯光，你可以看到数百乃至数千颗星星。那是一道令人入迷的景致。

一位特别的孩子曾有过这样的经历，并在很年轻的时候就作出了一个惊人的决定：无论花多少时间，一定要认出天空中的每一颗星星！

但有一个问题：她是一个女孩。

※※※

那时是 19 世纪晚期，很多工作只提供给男性——尤其是涉及数学和科学方面的工作。

这个名叫安妮·强普·坎农（Annie Jump Cannon）的年轻姑娘进了一所天文台工作，一栋建筑里安放着人们用来研究夜空的望远镜。

因为她是位姑娘，那里的男士告诉她，她永远不可能被提拔到"助手"以上的级别。那些"合适的"工作是为男性提供的。这种说法在现在看起来是不可思议的，但在那时却很正常。不仅仅在她所生活的美国是那样，在全世界都一样。

她的工作非常艰巨。她需要研发出一种能把整个夜空划分为多个区域的系统，并找到一种能够记录下每一丝光所在位置的方法。

---

① **entrance** [ɪnˈtræns] *adj.* 使人入神的、令人欣喜的
② **reserve** [rɪˈzɜːv] *n.* 储备、储存、自然保护区；*vt.* 储备、保留、预约；*vi.* 预订
③ **pinpoint** [ˈpɪnpɔɪnt] *vt.* 查明、精确地找到、准确描述；*adj.* 精确的、详尽的；*n.* 针尖、精确位置、极小之物

She also needed to write down what sort of light it was. Have you noticed, some stars are bright, while others are **dim**①? Also, some seem bigger than others. And some stars twinkle while others shine in a steady way. Some are slightly blue or a little bit red or have a yellow tint to them.

Annie Jump Cannon needed a system that would cover all **eventualities**②.

The work was quite **tedious**③, which meant that it needed careful, repetitive work. Most of the men did not have the patience to do this, so Annie and some of the other women ended up doing most of it.

She was so good at it that she became well known among the world community of astronomers.

After a few years, the **stargazing**④ community realized that Annie had identified an astonishing 500,000 stars — more than all the male astronomers in the world put together, in all of history!

What's more, her way of describing each star, known as her "**stellar**⑤ classification system", was considered so useful that astronomers all over the world, including in Europe and Asia, adopted it.

And that little girl who loved looking at the stars is remembered as the queen of the night sky.

她也需要记下光线的类型。你有没有注意到有些星星很亮，但有些却很暗？同样地，有些星星看起来比别的星星大。还有，有些星星一闪一闪的，有些却以稳定的方式发光。有些星星泛着蓝光，有些却泛着红光或是黄光。

安妮需要找到一个可以涵盖所有可能性的系统。

这项工作极其枯燥乏味，同时也意味着这是一项需要细心的重复性工作。大多数男性没有耐心去做这样的事，所以最后，安妮和其他女性完成了大部分工作。

安妮的工作非常出色，她在天文学界出了名。

在数年后，观星界的人士发现，安妮已经识别了 500 000 颗星星！这是一个惊人的数据，已经超过了历史上所有男性天文学家识别出的星星数量之和！

而且，人们认为，安妮记述星星的方法（称为"恒星分类系统"）非常实用，全世界（包括欧洲和亚洲在内）的天文学家都采用了这种方法。

热爱观察星星的小女孩安妮被称为"夜空女王"，为世人所铭记。

---

① **dim** [dɪm] *adj.* 暗淡的、昏暗的、模糊的、看不清的；*vt.* 使暗淡、使失去光泽、使变模糊；*vi.* 变模糊、变暗淡 [dimmer, dimmest, dimmed, dimmed, dimming]
② **eventuality** [ɪˌven(t)ʃʊˈælɪtɪ] *n.* 可能性、可能发生的事，不测的事 [eventualities]
③ **tedious** [ˈtiːdɪəs] *adj.* 沉闷的、冗长乏味的 [more tedious, most tedious]
④ **stargaze** [ˈstɑːɡeɪz] *vi.* 耽于幻想、眺望星辰 [stargazed, stargazed, stargazing]
⑤ **stellar** [ˈstelə] *adj.* 星的、星球的，主要的、一流的

THE BOY WHO UNDERSTOOD EINSTEIN

加来道雄
理解爱因斯坦的男孩

GROWN-UPS RARELY GET excited about things, but sometimes something in the news gets their attention.

An eight-year-old boy called Michio was intrigued when all the grown-ups started talking about a man called Albert Einstein who had just died.

This was 1955, and radio reports said Einstein discovered lots of things about the universe that were so complicated that most people would never be able to understand them.

Stars and planets had "**gravity wells**①" around them, and if you travelled at the speed of light to another galaxy and came back, time would have passed for you at a different rate compared to your family members who stayed at your home planet.

It was all eye-widening stuff!

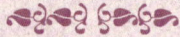

Michio Kaku, a boy born to an American family with Japanese roots, learned that the media called the man who had just died "a scientist", but Einstein preferred to call himself "an artist".

The white-haired genius worked more like an author, sitting at his desk thinking and writing.

Puzzled, Michio Kaku decided to study physics himself.

It was **tricky**② at first, but he found it fun — which often happens when you have a strong personal interest in a tough subject.

By the time Michio was a teenager, he was doing remarkable things. His contribution to a display of school projects was a **particle accelerator**③.

成年人很少对一般事物感到兴奋，但有时新闻中的一些事会吸引他们的注意力。

　　当所有成年人都在讨论一位刚刚去世的名叫爱因斯坦的男子时，这一切引起了八岁男孩加来道雄（Michio Kaku）的兴趣。

　　那年是 1955 年，收音机中的报道称，爱因斯坦发现了关于极其复杂的宇宙的许多奥秘，这些奥秘对大多数人来讲永远无法理解。

　　恒星和行星周围都存在"引力井"，如果你以光速在星系之间穿梭，你所度过的时间和你的家人在地球上度过的时间是不一样的。

　　这真是令人大开眼界！

　　加来道雄，这个出生在美国的日裔男孩，了解到媒体称死去的爱因斯坦为"科学家"，但事实上爱因斯坦更喜欢自称"艺术家"。

　　爱因斯坦——这位一头白发的天才工作时更像一位作家，他坐在书桌前思考、读写。

　　在迷茫中，加来道雄决定自学物理学。

　　开始时他感到物理学难以捉摸，但后来就发现了其中的乐趣——这通常发生在一个人对一门困难的学科产生强烈的兴趣时。

　　加来道雄十几岁时，他就做了很多不同寻常的事。他装配了一台粒子加速器，在学校的项目展示会上展出。

① **gravity well** 引力井，自流井
② **tricky** ['trɪkɪ] *adj.* 狡猾的、机警的 [trickier, trickiest]
③ **particle accelerator** 粒子加速器、质点加速器

Of course, it wasn't such a fancy one as the huge one in Europe (27 kilometers long) known as CERN, which makes lots of headlines in the newspapers.

But it did actually work.

Even most of the grown-ups visiting the school had no idea what a particle accelerator was, so Michio had to explain to them that if you used a machine to **slam**① invisibly small particles together, they would sometimes crack open and you could get interesting information about the basic elements which make up the universe.

The fact that a teenager was trying to detect or create **anti-matter**②, stuff that most other children would only encounter in comic books, got people's attention.

A working scientist took an interest in Michio and helped him get into good science universities, where he became a star student.

But it wasn't until Michio became an adult working as a science professor himself that he found the perfect job for himself.

Instead of working in labs, he decided that he would contribute more to society as an explainer of science.

And that's what he became. Today he is an author who writes books and **hosts**③ television shows teaching people about the wonders of physics.

当然，它比不上欧洲核子研究中心（CERN）的那个大型粒子加速器。欧洲的这个设备有 27 千米长，经常出现在报纸的头条上。

但是它确实很有用。

大多数成年人在参观学校时也都不知道粒子加速器是什么，所以加来道雄得向他们解释说，如果你用一种仪器猛击看不见的细小微粒，微粒有时会裂开，从而我们就能得到关于组成宇宙的基本元素的有趣信息。

一个少年正在设法侦测或创造大多数其他孩子有可能只在连环画中看到的反物质，这一点吸引了人们的注意。

一名科学家对加来道雄产生了兴趣，帮助他进入了一所很好的科研型大学。而加来道雄在大学中很快成为一位明星学生。

但是，加来道雄直到成年后成为一名科学教授，他才真正明白最适合自己的工作是什么。

他决定更多地投身于社会，成为一个向大众解释科学的人，而不只是埋头于实验室的工作中。

他确实那样做了。如今他是一名作家，写书并且主持电视节目，向人们展示物理学的神奇之处。

---

① **slam** [slæm] vt. 砰地关上、猛力抨击；vi. 砰地关上、猛力抨击 [slammed, slammed, slamming]
② **antimatter** ['æntɪˌmætə] n. 反物质
③ **host** [həʊst] n. [计] 主人、主持人；vt. 主持、当主人招待；vi. 群集、做主人

And yes, even today, one of the things he is often called on to do is to explain the discoveries of Einstein — and he can do it in such a way that even eight-year-olds can understand.

And maybe you, dear reader, may be inspired by this page to go from learning about scientists like Michio Kaku to being one yourself — and then the circle of life will continue to turn.

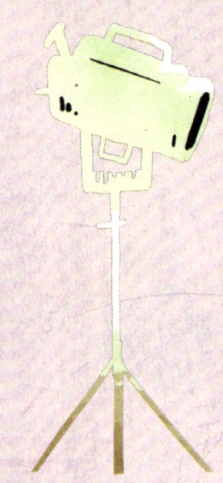

直到今日，他仍然经常被要求去做的一件事是：解释爱因斯坦所作出的发现。他的解释甚至能够让八岁的孩子听懂。

亲爱的读者，可能你也会因为这几页所讲述的故事而对加来道雄这样的科学家产生兴趣，想要成为这样的人。那么，你的人生也会从此而改变。

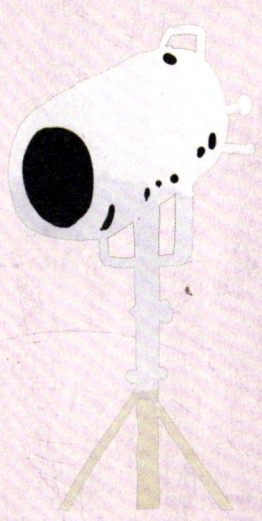

The Young Scientists Series:

Secrets in the Rocks and The Call of the Stars

by

Nury Vittachi

English Copyright © 2017 by World Scientific Publishing Co. Pte. Ltd.

Bi-lingual (Simplified Chinese & English) Character Copyright © 2018 by Shanghai Scientific & Technological Education Publishing House

Shanghai Scientific & Technological Education Publishing House published bi-lingual edition by arranged with World Scientific Publishing Co. Pte. Ltd., Singapore

All rights reserved. This book, or parts thereof, may not be reproduced in any form or by any means, electronic or mechanical, including photocopying, recording or any information storage and retrieval system now known or to be invented, without written permission from the Publisher.

ALL RIGHTS RESERVED

上海科技教育出版社业经World Scientific Publishing Co. Pte. Ltd.同意取得本书中英文双语版版权

责任编辑　侯慧菊
封面设计　杨　静

"伟人的少年故事"丛书
天地的秘密——观察星星和石头的科学家
［斯里兰卡］努雷·维塔奇（Nury Vittachi）　著
斯泰帕·张（Step Cheung）　图
朱之翀　译
张　群　审校

出版发行	上海科技教育出版社有限公司
	（上海市柳州路218号　邮政编码200235）
网　　址	www.ewen.co　www.sste.com
经　　销	各地新华书店
印　　刷	上海昌鑫龙印务有限公司
开　　本	889×1194　1/32
印　　张	3
版　　次	2018年8月第1版
印　　次	2018年8月第1次印刷
书　　号	ISBN 978-7-5428-6707-0/G·3833
图　　字	09-2017-937号
定　　价	25.00元

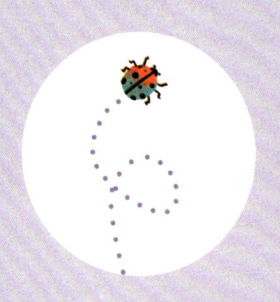

扫描二维码
获取教师参考资料
及练习答案

扫描二维码
获取学生练习册